THE ZULU

OF AFRICA

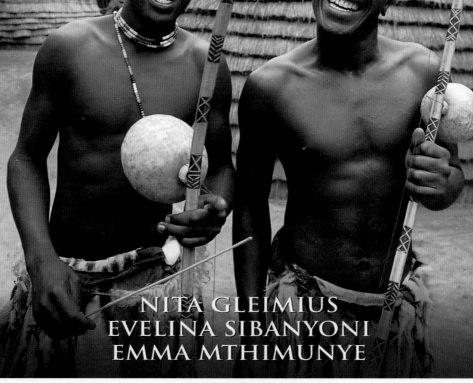

NITA GLEIMIUS
EVELINA SIBANYONI
EMMA MTHIMUNYE

Lerner Publications Company • Minneapolis

**First American edition published in 2003
by Lerner Publications Company**

Published by arrangement with Times Editions
Copyright © 2003 by Times Media Private Limited

Lerner Publications Company
A division of Lerner Publishing Group
241 First Avenue North
Minneapolis, MN 55401 U.S.A.
Website address: www.lernerbooks.com

Series originated and designed by
Times Editions
An imprint of Times Media Private Limited
A member of the Times Publishing Group
1 New Industrial Road, Singapore 536196
Website address: www.timesone.com.sg/te

Series editors: Margaret J. Goldstein, Yumi Ng
Series designers: Tuck Loong, Lynn Chin
Series picture researcher: Susan Jane Manuel

Library of Congress Cataloging-in-Publication Data
Gleimius, Nita.
The Zulu of Africa / by Nita Gleimius, Evelina Sibanyoni, and
Emma Mthimunye.
p. cm. — (First peoples)
Includes bibliographical references and index.
Summary: Describes the history, culture, modern and traditional
economies, religion, family life, and language of South Africa's
Zulu people, as well as the region in which they live.
ISBN 0-8225-0661-0 (lib. bdg. : alk. paper)
1. Zulu (African people)—Juvenile literature. [1. Zulu
(African people) 2. South Africa.] I. Sibanyoni, Evelina.
II. Mthimunye, Emma. III. Title. IV. Series.
CURR DT1768.Z95 G54 2003
968'.004963986—dc21   2002001394

Printed in Malaysia
Bound in the United States of America

1 2 3 4 5 6–OS–08 07 06 05 04 03

CONTENTS

WHO ARE THE ZULU?

The Zulu are a proud, handsome African people. For centuries, the Zulu had their own independent nation in the southern part of Africa. Their traditional territory, Zululand, is part of South Africa's KwaZulu-Natal Province. More than nine million Zulu people live in South Africa, and around seven million Zulu live in KwaZulu-Natal. Present-day Zulu are South African citizens and enjoy equal rights with South Africans of other groups and races. The Zulu still have a king and clan chiefs. These leaders play important roles in the government of KwaZulu-Natal.

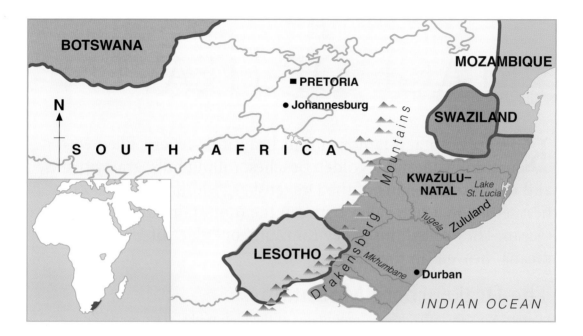

Modern Zulu Life

Modern Zulu people can be divided into three groups: traditional Zulu, semi-urbanized Zulu, and urbanized Zulu. Traditional Zulu live in KwaZulu-Natal's countryside. They follow the customs of their ancestors. They live in homes made of grass, mud, and sticks, although some of them build brick homes. Semi-urbanized Zulu are mostly men who have moved from the countryside to the city to find work. They usually live in dormitories but go home to their families on weekends and for vacations. These men have adopted some urban ways but still practice a lot of traditional customs, especially when they go home. Urbanized Zulu live in European-style homes in the city. Their lifestyle is very similar to that of American and European people. They speak English most of the time, but might also speak the Zulu language at home and teach their children Zulu folktales. But, as more Zulu become urbanized, the old customs might soon be lost.

RELATIVES OF THE ZULU

Two other African nations speak a language similar to Zulu. They are the Ndebele of northeastern South Africa and the Matabele of Zimbabwe. The Ndebele and the Zulu are both descendants of the Nguni, an ancient group of people who lived in the Great Lakes area of East Africa. The Matabele fled from the fierce King Shaka in the early 1800s. Their leader was a general named Mzilikazi.

PLACE OF HEAVEN

KwaZulu-Natal is famous for its beautiful scenery, filled with natural wilderness, golden beaches, rolling hills, grassy plains, and the purple heights of the Drakensberg Mountains. The Zulu first settled in a rich valley between the mountains and the Indian Ocean. They called this valley KwaZulu, or "place of Heaven" (*zulu* means "heaven" in their language).

The Drakensberg Mountains

Izintaba Zo Kahlamba means "mountains of the high peaks." That is the Zulu name for the Drakensberg Mountains. The Boers, descendants of Dutch settlers in South Africa, thought that the rugged mountain ridges resembled a gigantic dragon. They named the mountains Drakensberg, which means "dragon mountains" in Dutch.

Below: The scenic Champagne Castle Valley in the central Drakensberg Mountains

Above: Durban, in KwaZulu-Natal, is famous for its sandy beaches, which stretch for miles along the coast.

The Midlands

The Midlands sit between the coast and the Drakensberg Mountains. This fertile area holds valleys, plains, hills, and fast-flowing rivers. The Zulu first settled in the Midlands, where there was plenty of grazing land for their cattle.

The Coastal Region

KwaZulu-Natal stretches along the Indian Ocean for many miles. Warm ocean currents bring showers to the coast almost every afternoon of the year.

LAKE ST. LUCIA

Lake St. Lucia is part of Great Zululand Wetlands Park. The lake is 25 miles (40 kilometers) long and 6 miles (10 kilometers) wide. It is quite shallow—only around 6 feet 5 inches (2 meters) deep. The lake is home to many crocodiles, hippos (*above*), and 350 different kinds of birds, along with many other wild animals and plants. When visitors see the large crocodiles sunbathing on the banks of the lake, they do not hesitate to obey the "Swimming Not Allowed" signs at the lake.

THE PLANTS OF ZULULAND

KwaZulu-Natal has plentiful and varied plant life. The Zulu use native plants and trees to build their houses and to make other useful items. Zulu healers use many wild plants and herbs to cure illnesses and heal wounds. The government has set up nature preserves, game parks, and wilderness trails to protect the province's native plants and animals.

Left: An elegant giraffe reaches up for its food. The fertile land of KwaZulu-Natal provides plenty of food for wild animals.

Great Zululand Wetlands Park

This nature preserve consists of a natural forest next to about 50 miles (80 kilometers) of sandy, unspoiled beach. The park also contains coastal sand dunes. Some of them are more than 656 feet (200 meters) high—some of the highest dunes in the world. There about 175 species of trees here, including lala palms and mangrove trees. The park is home to a multitude of wildlife.

Forests and Trees

Wild banana plants and date palm trees grow near the KwaZulu-Natal coast. Deciduous trees—trees that shed their leaves every year—grow in the beautiful Injasuti Valley. Many kinds of wildflowers and shrubs also grow in the province. In some rural areas, the Zulu use the fire-resistant paperbark tree to build fences.

Grasslands

Red grass, buffalo grass, elephant grass, and many other grasses grow abundantly in the Midlands and foothills of KwaZulu-Natal. The Zulu use strong, long grasses to build their homes and to weave baskets, ropes, and sleeping mats. The shorter grasses of the Midlands are ideal food for cattle.

Above: Rural Zulu use trees to build fences for their homes.

Below: A Zulu woman weaves a mat from grasses found in the forest.

FOREIGN SPECIES

European settlers, arriving in KwaZulu-Natal in the 1800s, destroyed large areas of grassland and forest to make way for farms and orchards. The settlers planted pine, wattle, and other foreign trees in place of the native plants. The wood from these trees was used to make furniture, matches, paper, and other products. In modern times, the national and provincial governments have set aside numerous nature preserves in KwaZulu-Natal to protect the native plants.

ZULULAND ANIMALS

L ess than a hundred years ago, wild animals roamed all over KwaZulu-Natal. But, over the years, people built farms, towns, and roads throughout the province. In modern times, animals can no longer freely roam the countryside. Many wild animals live in nature preserves, where they are protected from human interference.

Animals on Land

The area's herbivores, or plant-eating animals, include large numbers of antelopes, kudus, reedbucks, blue wildebeests, monkeys, zebras, warthogs, buffaloes, giraffes, elephants, and white and black rhinoceroses. Carnivores, or meat-eating animals, include leopards, lions, jackals, and hyenas. Hyenas are the "garbage collectors" of the animal world. They eat the leftover food of other animals.

Below: A zebra and her young roam the vast grasslands of KwaZulu-Natal.

Left: The king-fisher is one of the many birds found in the coastal areas of Zululand.

Birds in the Air

More than 200 different kinds of birds, including the rare lammergeier, a kind of vulture, as well as eagles and other vultures live in the Drakensberg Mountains. Wetland and coastal areas have more than 350 different kinds of birds, including pelicans, flamingos, blue and wattled cranes, wild ducks, geese, and kingfishers. When thousands of beautiful butterflies hatch there, the Ngoye Forest turns into a fairy garden.

Below: The elegant pink flamingo is a common sight in the wetlands of KwaZulu-Natal.

Water Creatures

The marshes here teem with all kinds of fish and other water creatures. The swamps around Lake St. Lucia are home to barbels and tiger fish. From June to September, whales swim down the coast of the Indian Ocean. Sharks are plentiful, too. Oyster beds flourish off the province's north coast. Dolphins play in the blue waters off the north of Durban.

GIANT SEA TURTLES

On warm November nights, giant sea turtles struggle onto the beaches of Zululand. There they dig holes in the sand with their hind legs, deposit their eggs, scratch the sand back into the holes, and slowly waddle back to the water. Some of these turtles are 7 feet (2.13 meters) long and can weigh 1,200 pounds (544 kilograms)! When baby turtles hatch, they dig out of their sandy nests and make their way to the water. Seagulls and other predators swoop down to feast on the tiny turtles. Only a small percentage of them reach the water safely.

ZULU ORIGINS

The Zulu nation is a proud one. The nation started off as a large family, or clan, with a small group of followers. In the early 1800s, under the leadership of the legendary King Shaka, the Zulu became one of the mightiest nations in Africa.

Ancestors of the Zulu

According to Zulu tales, around three thousand years ago, a group of people migrated south with their cattle from Egypt. They traveled along the shores of the Red Sea and settled near the Great Lakes of East Africa. The people and their cattle grew in number. Some families split off from the main group and moved southeast toward the Indian Ocean. These people had to change their lifestyle to suit their new environment. But they always remembered their origins through songs and stories.

Below: This painting found in a cave at Giant's Castle in the Drakensberg Mountains depicts early African life. Here, a man is carrying two reedbucks he has killed.

KwaZulu– Place of Heaven

Around three hundred years ago, one small family group, led by a young chief named Zulu (his name means "heaven"), settled in the lush valley of the Mkhumbane River. As time went by, the Zulu family and its followers increased. The settlement became a village, and the family became a clan. Until the late 1700s, the Zulu clan led a peaceful life. Then powerful Chief Dingiswayo of the Mtetwa clan convinced Chief Senzangakhona of the Zulu to join him in battle against nearby clans.

The Warrior King

The fight continued under the next Zulu leader, Shaka, Senzangakhona's illegitimate son. He took over the clan in 1815 and started building an army. A year later, after the Ndwandwe clan defeated Dingiswayo's armies, Shaka attacked and defeated the Nwandwe. He took over their land and possessions. By the time of his death in 1828, Shaka had built the small Zulu clan into a mighty empire. The land of the Zulu stretched over a vast area, from the Tugela River in the south to the Mozambique border in the north.

Below: An illustration of King Shaka wearing military attire

THE AFRICAN NAPOLÉON

Shaka was a brilliant military man and a ruthless warrior. He has been compared to Napoléon Bonaparte, the great French general and emperor. Shaka invented a short spear and a small, easy-to-handle shield. Both weapons later helped his army win many battles. Shaka trained his army with ferocious discipline, punishing even the smallest offense with death. In the end, his brutality won him many enemies. In 1828 his half-brother Dingane, cooperating with other members of the royal family, murdered Shaka.

13

THE COLONIAL ERA

Up to the 1800s, the Zulu had very little contact with Europeans. In 1497 the Portuguese explorer Vasco da Gama had reached Zululand on Christmas Day. Da Gama named the region Natal, which means "Christmas" in Portuguese, but he did not stay long. The British established a small trading post at Port Natal (modern-day Durban) in 1824. Gradually, the Zulu began to meet European traders and missionaries. The Zulu gave the Europeans food in exchange for tin utensils, cloth, and colored glass beads.

European Settlers

The fertile and beautiful Natal countryside attracted European settlers. In the 1830s, Dutch settlers called Boers sent their leader, along with 100 men, to buy land from Zulu King Dingane. The king tricked the Boer men and killed them and their families. The Boers then sent an army to avenge this brutal killing. They defeated the Zulu army at the Battle of Blood River in 1838. When his messengers told Dingane the news of the defeat, he fled to Swaziland. He was murdered shortly afterward by his own people. His half-brother Mpande succeeded him.

Below: Zulu warriors fight against British troops at Ginghilovo in 1879.

Mpande and Cetshwayo

King Mpande reigned for thirty years. In 1872 Mpande's son Cetshwayo became the new Zulu king. While Cetshwayo was king, British soldiers invaded Zulu territory. After many fierce battles, the British defeated the Zulu and captured Cetshwayo. In 1879 Zululand was annexed to the British colony of Natal. The British divided the Zulu nation into small kingdoms, each with a Zulu chief. The British sent Cetshwayo back to Natal to oversee all kingdoms.

Left: King Cetshwayo was captured by the British and sent to England, where he met Queen Victoria.

SECRET PLACE OF THE ELEPHANT

King Dingane—"Great Elephant"—built a new Zulu capital. He called it Mgungundlovo, which means "secret place of the elephant." The city held about seven thousand people and about 1,700 beehive (dome-shaped) huts. Europeans, mostly traders and missionaries, were allowed to visit the city, as long as they brought gifts to the king. The Europeans described the people of Mgungundlovo, moving about their daily business, as "busy ants among a maze of beehive homes."

FROM APARTHEID TO DEMOCRACY

B ritish rulers introduced the Zulu nation to European customs. But the Zulu nation, although defeated, did not give way completely to British rule. A king and clan chiefs continued to rule small areas. But Europeans took over almost all the farmland in KwaZulu-Natal. They took control of government and businesses.

The Apartheid Era

South Africa became a self-governing country in 1910. Although the majority of the nation's people were black, the leaders were almost all white. Many of the leaders did not want blacks and whites to mix. In 1948 the government passed a law that forced the African nations to live in separate territories called homelands. The Zulu and other black peoples could not live in white areas. This system of separating the races is called apartheid. By the 1950s, most black South Africans lived in poverty, while many of the white minority lived comfortable lives. Many people in South Africa disagreed with the system.

Below: A park in South Africa reserved for white people in the 1950s

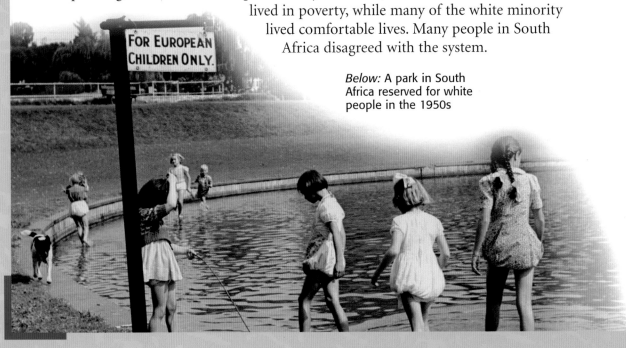

The Rainbow Nation

In the early 1990s, after years of criticism from around the world, change finally came to South Africa. Apartheid was ended, and a new Republic of South Africa was born. Under a new constitution, all people are equal in modern-day South Africa. The new constitution also allows the Zulu nation to have a king.

Above: After the 1994 elections, all South Africans— black and white— enjoy equal rights.

A ZULU HERO

Chief Mangosuthu Buthelezi (*left*) has been a leader in the fight for Zulu rights. He is a descendant of Zulu, the nation's first chief. He was head of the Inkhata Freedom Party, a group that fought to end apartheid. Buthelezi believed in fighting injustice peacefully. In 1994 he became minister of home affairs in the Republic of South Africa.

IN THE WAY OF THE ANCESTORS

I n the KwaZulu-Natal countryside, Zulu people still live like their ancestors did. Older Zulu still work as farmers and cattle herders. Many younger Zulu, however, prefer to move to the cities to look for jobs.

Zulu Farmers

In rural villages, Zulu farmers raise mostly corn, barley, and sorghum. They produce just enough vegetables and grain to feed their families. In other rural areas, many Zulu own or work on large sugarcane plantations, fruit orchards, or dairy farms.

Trade

Traditionally, the Zulu clans and tribes practiced barter, or the exchange of goods. After the arrival of the Europeans, the Zulu continued to trade food and animal skins in exchange for beads, copper wire, and cloth. Present-day Zulu exchange goods for money. They sell wares, fruit, and vegetables at small farm stalls are located along tourist routes.

Left: A rural Zulu woman clears weeds from her cabbage field in KwaZulu-Natal.

THE IMPORTANCE OF CATTLE

The Zulu love their cattle (*left*). Every animal has a name, and a Zulu farmer can tell each animal in the herd apart from a thousand others. Zulu men spend hours watching their cattle, getting to know the looks of each animal. Among traditional Zulu, cattle are a sign of wealth and status. A man with many cattle has a lot of power in his village.

Cattle Herding

Traditional Zulu are cattle herders. Boys learn to herd cattle at a very young age. Early in the morning, boys milk the cows and take herds to the fields to graze. In the late afternoon, the boys drive the cattle back to a kraal, an enclosure located in the middle of the village. There, the boys milk the cows again.

Below: A modern-day Zulu plows his field with the help of cattle.

THE MODERN ECONOMY

In recent years, the Zulu economy has started to change. Some modern Zulu farm on a larger scale, using powerful machines. Instead of raising animals and crops only for their own needs, these farmers sell meat, milk, and crops in South Africa's cities. Tourism and other industries are also important to the Zulu.

Welcoming Visitors

KwaZulu-Natal is a paradise of natural beauty. Nature preserves, mountain resorts, and beaches are popular tourist spots. Many Zulu work at nature preserves. Many tourists also like to visit Zulu villages to learn about the traditional Zulu way of life. The villagers sell homemade products to these tourists. They demonstrate traditional skills such as basket weaving, pottery, leatherworking, woodcarving, and beadworking. Zulu crafts are also exported and sold around the world.

Below: A group of tourists gets a close look at traditional Zulu life.

Mining and Other Jobs

In the late 1800s and early 1900s, many Zulu men left KwaZulu-Natal to work in coal, diamond, and gold mines. They stayed in hostels in the cities and visited their families during holidays. Some Zulu still work in the mines, but others work in many different fields. They hold jobs at sugar mills, oil refineries, and automobile assembly plants. There are also many Zulu professionals, such as doctors and lawyers, in South Africa.

Above: A Zulu man works in a gold mine.

CULTURAL TOURISM

Some Zulu have opened up their homes and villages to tourists who want to learn about traditional Zulu culture. The villagers offer unusual vacation packages. Tourists sleep on reed mats in old-fashioned beehive huts. They eat traditional Zulu meals cooked over open fires. The most famous Zulu tourist village is Shakaland (*left*).

A ZULU VILLAGE

The traditional Zulu village is called an *umuzi*. Each village is home to one clan, or large family group. The typical village has between five and twenty families.

The Village Plan

The Zulu village is round or oval. It has two fences, one inside the other. The Zulu build huts and other buildings between the two fences. The largest hut is built opposite the entrance to the village. This hut belongs to the mother of the chief. The chief's hut sits to the right of his mother's home. Unmarried teenage girls live together in a large hut on the left side of the entrance to the village. Unmarried teenage boys live to the right of the entrance. Small huts sitting on poles serve as watchtowers and food storage facilities. There is also a brewery, where women brew *tshwala*, traditional Zulu beer.

Above: The Zulu store food in huts above ground, which keeps the food safe from animals.

Below: A small-scale reproduction of a traditional Zulu village

Above: A modern-day Zulu village. Most Zulu villages are located on a small hill.

Finding the Right Place

The Zulu like to build their villages on small hills. They build the entrance to the village at the low end of the hill. That way, rainwater will run down the hill through the cattle kraal, cleaning it quickly without soaking the ground and huts. In the old days, there was another very important reason for building a village on a slope. The hill protected the villagers against attacks, as the enemy had to fight uphill to overtake the village.

The Cattle Kraal

Cattle kraals, or *izibaya*, are located in the center of the village, within the inner fence. A small enclosure houses the calves. The kraal also has underground storage pits for grain. The cattle kraal is the safest and most important area in the village. It is used for religious ceremonies, and sometimes as a burial place for chiefs.

ROYAL GATEKEEPERS

The chief's two eldest sons work as the village gatekeepers (*left*). They welcome important visitors immediately and send unwanted visitors away. After visitors enter the village, the gatekeepers treat them to a ritual of singing. The boys' songs praise their father's achievements. Gatekeeping is part of a future chief's training, since gatekeepers get to know their father's guests and how they should be treated.

TRADITIONAL ZULU HOMES

Traditional Zulu homes are beehive-shaped huts called *iQukwane*. In many villages, homes still resemble beehives, but they are sometimes built using modern materials such as brick and tin. A *rondawel* is a modern-day Zulu hut. The roof of a rondawel is made from grasses but its walls are built using bricks.

Building the Hut

To build a traditional hut, men collect strong young tree branches. They place the branches in a circle the size of the hut. They bend the branches together at the top to form a roof. In the center, they place a strong pole or tree trunk for support. Zulu women make the walls from braided grass, split reeds, and a mud mixture. This mixture makes the hut waterproof.

Left: A Zulu hut under construction. Zulu women are responsible for weaving the walls of the hut.

Above: A Zulu man selects suitable bamboo branches to make the walls of a hut.

A Floor That Will Last a Lifetime

Zulu women mix wet cattle dung with finely chopped anthills to make a thick, smooth paste. They spread this mixture inside the hut to make a floor. When the mixture is dry, it becomes as hard as rock. The women polish the floor with a stone until it is as shiny and smooth as glass. A small area of the floor, near the central pole, is used as a fireplace.

AN IDEAL HOME

Zulu huts (*left*) are cool in summer and warm in winter. They are easy to construct—the rich forests of KwaZulu-Natal provide an abundant supply of free building material. Smoke from the fireplace can escape through the door and a hole in the roof. The smoke helps to keep bugs out of the home.

LIFE IN A ZULU VILLAGE

Every Zulu clan lives in a separate village. Everybody in the village is related. Each village has a chief. Zulu society is patriarchal, meaning that the men make all the decisions.

Women's Jobs

Zulu women care for the children, prepare food, and serve meals to their husbands. Women also tend crops, carry water, and make crafts. Although women do not have direct authority, they can still influence the men in their families. Zulu grandmothers are greatly honored.

Above: At a young age, Zulu women learn to balance pots filled with water.

Leaders and Warriors

Zulu men make all the decisions concerning the family and the clan. The man owns all the family possessions. In the days when the Zulu battled with other African nations and Europeans, Zulu men trained to be warriors. Modern Zulu no longer fight wars, but they still must be able to defend their families.

Below: Rural Zulu sometimes settle disputes by stick fighting.

Above: Modern Zulu children are taught the traditional Zulu customs by their grandparents.

Zulu Children

From a very young age, Zulu children learn to respect their elders. Children speak only when they are spoken to. Children change their names several times during childhood. At birth they get baby names. Boys are named by their fathers when they turn seven, and again by their friends when they herd cattle. In past eras, boys got their final names when they joined a regiment, or *amabutho*, and became warriors. Zulu girls are also named by their fathers and finally by their friends.

HONORED GRANDPARENTS

Grandparents (*left*) have a special place in Zulu society. Grandfathers, no matter how old, must be consulted in all matters concerning the family. Grandparents are also the teachers of Zulu traditions. They repeat the ancient stories exactly as they learned them from their own grandparents. Before a grandparent starts to tell a story, he or she performs a ceremony by the fire.

LIVING ZULU CULTURE

Rural Zulu and even some urban Zulu still follow many of the customs of their ancestors faithfully.

Greeting, Walking, and Giving

If two Zulu people meet, the person with a higher social status, such as an elder or chief, will greet the other person first by saying "Sawubona" ("I see you"). The other person responds, "Yebo, sawubona" ("Yes, I see you too"). The Zulu avoid eye contact, as it is a sign of disrespect to look a superior in the eyes. Women usually walk behind men so that men can protect them from danger. Objects are always passed with the right hand, supported at the elbow by the left hand.

Below: The Zulu must follow many social rules whenever they interact with one another.

28

Bride Payment

A bridegroom must give his future father-in-law a payment, or *lobola*. The lobola is meant to repay the father for money he spent raising his daughter. It also pays for the loss of her help in his household. Traditionally, the bride payment is made in cattle. In cities, the payment is made in cash. If the bride does not perform her household duties well after marriage, the bridegroom can demand a refund from his father-in-law in the form of cash or cattle.

Above: Even in the cities, the payment given to the bride's father by her bridegroom must be equal to a certain number of cattle.

EAR PIERCING

Traditional Zulu pierce the ears of both males and females (*right*). They first make a tiny hole in the earlobe and insert a small object to keep it open. Larger and larger objects are inserted over a period of time. This practice is said "to open the ears of the mind."

TRADITIONAL ZULU FOOD

The rural Zulu diet is mostly vegetarian. The Zulu love meat, but they eat it only on special occasions. They cook and serve food in big black metal pots. They used to eat from wooden plates, but in modern times they mostly use tin or glass plates. The Zulu often drink tshwala, or beer, along with their meals. It is served from a hollowed-out calabash, a kind of gourd.

Daily Meals

Traditionally, Zulu families ate two meals a day. The first meal was eaten around mid-morning, and the second was eaten before bedtime. Favorite Zulu foods include boiled and pounded corn, toasted corncobs, sour milk, boiled sweet potatoes, mashed pumpkin, cabbage and sorghum porridge, and a crumbly porridge made from cornmeal. In the evening, the Zulu often eat porridge with a thick sauce made from tomatoes and onions.

Right: Traditional handmade Zulu cooking utensils. Zulu women grind corn and other foods using a stone board and roller.

Cleaning with Ashes

The Zulu are very clean when preparing food. They scour pots with ashes to keep them spotless. Sometimes they rub ashes on their teeth before rinsing their mouths. Ashes make their teeth sparkling white.

Left: A Zulu woman prepares porridge to feed the whole family.

Left: A man eats porridge using traditional Zulu eating utensils.

Mealtime Etiquette

People eat meals while squatting or sitting on the ground. Hands must be thoroughly washed before meals. Guests must never refuse any food that is offered to them. Rubbing the stomach, with a burp or two, shows appreciation for the food and drink. Guests must drink beer along with their hosts. Food is always served to the men first, then to the women, then to the boys, and last to the girls.

Right: Women carry cabbages they have picked. They will keep some for their families and sell the rest roadside stalls.

A SPECIAL DISH

Amazi is a Zulu delicacy. It is made by allowing milk to go sour until it curdles. The liquid that separates from the curdled milk is removed through a hole at the base of the container. This process is repeated until the milk becomes as thick as jelly. Although the Zulu gladly share food with guests, this dish is so precious that they share it only with family members.

TRADITIONAL ZULU WEAR

Zulu clothing has changed greatly in the past few decades. Traditionally, the Zulu used animal skins to make skirts. However, hunting for game has been restricted, so animal skins are no longer freely available. Rural Zulu must make their clothes using modern fabrics. Most urban Zulu wear modern-style clothes but wear traditional attire on special occasions.

Men's Clothing

Traditionally, Zulu men did not cover their upper bodies. They wore a short front apron made of round pieces of skin sewn together. A back apron was made out of soft calfskin. Long animal skins called *inJobo* were sometimes worn from the hips. Men also tied cow tails around their upper arms and below their knees to bulge out their muscles.

Below: The back apron worn by Zulu men was knee length for young men and ankle length for older men.

Left: Girls decorate their skirts with colorful beads that hang from the waist.

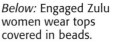

Below: Engaged Zulu women wear tops covered in beads.

Women's Wear

Traditionally, single Zulu girls wore short grass skirts. Present-day Zulu girls wear skirts made of different fabrics. When girls are old enough for courtship, they wear beads in their hair. Engaged girls add breast coverings to their red skirts. Married women wear long skirts, traditionally made of animal skin and colored black with charcoal. Pregnant women wear an extra apron of antelope skin, which the Zulu believe will empower the baby with grace and strength. Babies wear only a string of beads.

MAGNIFICENT HAIRDOS

Married women wear a magnificent hat-type hairpiece called an *isiCholo* (*left*). It is a grass and cotton headdress sewn into the hair. It resembles the bottom of a saucer turned upside down. It can be more than 3 feet (90 centimeters) across. When fixed properly, this hairdo can last for a few months. It then has to be redone. Women from different clans wear different styles of isiCholos.

ZULU ARTS AND CRAFTS

Scholars believe that Zulu artwork once carried stories from the distant past. They think that the symbols used to decorate crafts carried secret or special information. Some Zulu beadwork and baskets are still used to pass on messages.

The Art of Weaving

The Zulu weave beautiful baskets and sleeping mats. Traditional baskets are made from clay and grass. The pattern on a basket says something about the basket's owner or maker. For example, a basket with a triangle pattern indicates that the owner is a man. One with a diamond pattern means the owner is a woman. A basket with a check pattern is meant to wish the receiver good crops, good health, or many cattle.

Bead Art

The ancestors of the Zulu used beads made of wood and seeds. Arab and European traders introduced glass beads to Africa. The beads quickly became very valuable. They were traded for food and other items. Zulu women string hundreds of tiny beads into complex patterns of colors and shapes. They weave the beads to make necklaces, head coverings, loincloths, bracelets, anklets, and short skirts. The Zulu also decorate items such as pots, spoons, and calabashes with beads.

Left: Zulu women have perfected the art of bead weaving.

Beautiful Clay Pots

Zulu women are trained from a young age to make perfectly smooth clay pots by hand. They do not use potter's wheels. They bake the pots in a grass or dung fire. The fuel used for the fire affects the final color of the pot. The pots are beautifully decorated.

Left: The Zulu use beautiful pots to carry water and brew beer.

Wood and Stone Carving

Zulu men used to carve eating utensils, headrests, pails, and other useful items from wood and stone. They occasionally made animal carvings, especially cattle. Present-day Zulu carvers make artwork mostly to sell to tourists and to export to other countries. The artwork includes beautiful carvings of wild animals, from very small to very large. The Zulu rarely carve household items anymore, as they can easily buy these items ready-made.

LOVE LETTERS

Zulu girls weave tiny squares of beads (*right, second from the front*) to show their suitors whether they like them or not. The message is given through the colors and patterns formed by the beads. Sometimes girls string small pieces of cloth, feathers, and leather together with the beads. The beads' colors have slightly different meanings in different areas of Zululand. White usually represents purity, and red indicates love. Black can mean sadness or anger.

ZULU MUSIC

The people of Africa love music, and the Zulu nation is no exception. Zulu men working in the mines developed their own musical style. They sang a cappella, or without instruments. Ladysmith Black Mambazo is a famous a cappella Zulu group.

The Gourd Bow

The *ugubhu,* also called the gourd bow, is made by stretching a string between two ends of a wooden bow, with a movable gourd attached. Musicians produce sounds by striking the string with a thin stick. They create different tones by moving the gourd up and down the bow.

Right: Zulu solo singers used to play the ugubhu to accompany their singing.

Left: Zulu drums are made from hollow containers covered with stretched animal skins.

The Zulu Drum— iziGubhu

The Zulu and other African people believe that the sound of drums can calm a restless person. Another drumbeat can prompt a cowardly person to run fearlessly into battle.

Sounds of Heaven

Zulu means "heaven," and Zulu choral singing can really sound like a chorus of heavenly angels. The Zulu are good at blending many voices and songs. They often sing up to five different parts together, with each singer contributing different words, melody, and rhythm.

Above: A Zulu female church choir

Wind Instruments

The traditional Zulu flute is called *umtshingo*. Musicians produce sounds by blowing at one end of the flute and stopping and unstopping the other end with a finger. A tin recorder called a *kivela* is popular with Zulus in the city.

A SINGING CONVERSATION

Groups of Zulu practice a "call and response" type of singing. The leader sings the verse of a song. A choir sings a refrain, or chorus. The leader then sings another verse, again followed by the choir. This pattern is repeated throughout the song. Solo singers like to sing call and response with a musical instrument, usually a guitar (*right*). The song sounds like a conversation between the singer and his or her musical instrument.

THE ZULU LANGUAGE

IsiZulu, the Zulu language, belongs to the Bantu group of central and eastern African languages. It is a smooth and pleasant-sounding language. It is a tonal language, which means that the speaker's tone, or pitch, can often determine a word's meaning. Traditionally, the Zulu did not have a written language. All their history, legends, and beliefs were passed down through storytelling. Later, after Europeans arrived in South Africa, IsiZulu was written down.

Below: The Zulu language is now written using the Roman alphabet. Signs in both English and IsiZulu can be seen in KwaZulu-Natal.

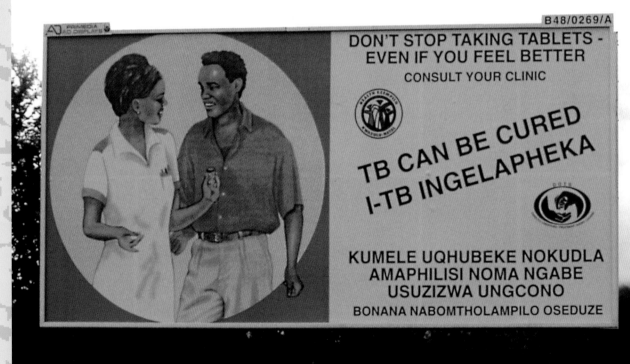

ZULU STORYTELLING

For hundreds of years, the Zulu have gathered their children around the fire at night and told stories. These stories pass on the Zulu language, values, history, religion, and legends. Modern Zulu children in the cities learn mostly from books and school. But in the rural villages, the tradition of storytelling survives. A grandparent (*left*) or an older member of the family is usually the storyteller. Before beginning the story, the storyteller performs a special ritual with snuff, a powder made from tobacco leaves. During this ritual, the storyteller promises the Zulu ancestors that the story will be repeated faithfully, in exactly the same manner that it was learned during childhood.

Learn to Speak IsiZulu

In Zulu, the second to the last syllable is usually stressed. The Zulu language has three "click" sounds not found in English. They are represented by the letters "c," "q," and "x." The sound is made by pressing the tip of the tongue firmly against the front part of the roof of the mouth, and then withdrawing it sharply with a noisy click. The prefix *isi* usually makes a noun singular, while *izi* makes it plural. Here are a few IsiZulu words:

Zulu	Pronunciation	English
intombazana	een-tawm-bah-ZAH-nah	girl
isiCholo	ee-see-tqaw-law	headdress
izikomo	ee-zee-nkaw-maw	cattle
umfana/abafana	oom-FAH-nah/ ah-bah-FAH-nah	boy/boys

ZULU RELIGION

Traditional Zulu worshipped their ancestors. They also believed in a supreme god called Nkulunkulu. Because of the European influence in South Africa, a large number of Zulu have converted to Christianity in the last hundred years. But many Zulu who converted still maintained their old beliefs. Many have combined traditional Zulu beliefs with the teachings of their adopted religion.

The Greatest of the Great

Traditional Zulu believe that Nkulunkulu—"the Greatest of the Great"— created all things. He created everything and everyone perfectly, without sickness or flaws. The Zulu believe that their god does not involve himself in small issues. He is concerned only with matters of life and death. Whenever a natural disaster takes place, such as a flood or an earthquake, Zulu believe that someone is trying to do them harm. They do not attribute the disaster to Nkulunkulu, since he created a perfect world.

Below: A rural Zulu Christian church

Worshipping the Ancestors

Traditional Zulu believe that a person's spirit continues to live even after death and that the spirit has the same authority he or she had during life. Thus, the spirit of a dead king will watch over his whole nation, while an ordinary person's spirit will watch over only his or her family. The Zulu give thanks to their ancestors whenever good things happen to them. If bad things happen, the Zulu believe that an ancestor has found fault in them. The Zulu often pour beer on the ground or leave bread next to a hut as a gift for the ancestors.

Above: Traditional Zulu sometimes sacrifice a white animal, such as a white cow, goat, or horse, to pacify an angry spirit.

THE SPIRIT WORLD

The Zulu believe that the spirits of their ancestors live in the world of Nkulunkulu. The ancestors are the link between the living world and the spirit world. The Zulu believe that spirits also dwell in animals, forests, and caves. The Zulu hold a special festival for a female spirit in the spring, as they believe she makes the crops grow (*right*).

SPIRITS AND WITCH DOCTORS

Zulu people are very superstitious. They believe that all bad things, such as accidents and nightmares, come from evil spirits that want to harm them. The Zulu try to avoid misfortune by practicing certain rituals.

River Spirits

Tokoloshe are small, evil creatures, supposedly created from the bodies of dead people. They are said to dwell among the reeds by rivers. Another nasty river spirit is an elf called Ichanti. Ichanti can change into a snake and then possess, or control, people. Before crossing a river, the Zulu throw stones into the water and make loud noises to scare Ichanti away.

Above: Before a storm, Zulu men sometimes burn herbs and beg the spirits to protect their village from lightning.

An Ancestor's Curse

According to Zulu belief, an ancestor's curse can cause lightning to strike a village. The Zulu will not mourn or hold a proper funeral for a person killed by lightning. They are not allowed to eat the meat of an animal killed by lightning or use the wood of a tree that has been struck by lightning.

Below: Traditional Zulu believe that some evil spirits live near riverbanks.

Traditional Doctors

There are three kinds of traditional Zulu doctors. Witch doctors can determine the cause of misfortune, protect people from evil spirits, and interpret omens. A person must go through special training to become a witch doctor. Herbal doctors, or medicine men, heal the sick using plants and herbs. The job is a hereditary position—the secrets of herbal medicine are passed down from parent to child. The "heaven doctor" or "sky herd" can control the weather and other natural events, and he protects people from thunder, lightning, and hail. He gets his power through magic.

Above: A female witch doctor teaches her apprentice to read the future by using bones.

NATURE'S ANTIBIOTICS

Zulu medicine men used antibiotics long before they were used in modern medicine. They treated dirty wounds with a mixture made from boiled leaves and dry badgers' urine. (The badger is a small mountain animal that resembles a rabbit.) The medicine man first called on the spirits three times while holding a mouthful of this liquid. He then squirted the liquid into the wound through a reed straw. Finally, he covered the wound with more leaves. The leaves drew dirt out of the wound. When given at the right time, this treatment saved many lives.

ZULU FESTIVALS

Zulu festivals are celebrations filled with song, dance, and lots of food. The men drink lots of tshwala, the traditional Zulu beer.

Below: Young Zulu men perform a warrior dance during a festival.

Right: Zulu princess Agnes is escorted by her bridesmaids on her wedding day.

The Wedding Feast

When a wedding takes place, the whole community gets together to celebrate. The wedding takes place in the groom's village. On the wedding day, groups of dancers celebrate by singing and dancing from early morning. Young women dance gently and modestly. Married women dance vigorously. Engaged girls dance boldly, with pebbles rattling in cans tied around their ankles. Older women wave branches. Young men dress in traditional warrior attire. Family groups trade good-natured insults, as the family of the bride must show resistance at the idea of losing a daughter. Each group dances to its own music, its own beat, its own noise, yet everything seems to blend together. The bride symbolically cuts ties with her past by carrying her sleeping mat and other goods into the groom's hut. The festivities carry on through the night. The wedding is officially over when the bridesmaids take the bride for a bath in the morning.

Below: A group of Zulu girls sing and dance during a Zulu celebration in Johannesburg.

THE ANNUAL REED DANCE

Once a year, young Zulu women, wearing traditional grass skirts and colorful beads and holding long reed strands upright, dance for the king. The king may use this occasion to choose a wife from among the dancers. The current Zulu king, King Goodwill Zwelithini, chose a wife during this festival.

GLOSSARY

ancestor: a person from whom one is descended

apartheid: the South African system of segregating, or separating, the races. Apartheid ended in 1994.

Boers: early Dutch, French, and German settlers in South Africa

carnivores: meat-eating animals

clan: a group of people tracing descent from a common ancestor

deciduous trees: trees that lose their leaves each year

descendants: a person's children and grandchildren

etiquette: rules of social behavior

herbivores: plant-eating animals

hereditary: passed down from parent to child

homelands: regions created by South Africa's apartheid government as homes for black tribes. Tribes were forced to relocate to the homelands.

illegitimate: a child born to parents who are not married to each other

kraal: an enclosed space for keeping cattle and other animals

migration: movement of people from their country of origin to another land

missionaries: religious teachers who try to convert others to their faith

nature preserves: large areas of wilderness set aside by the government to protect plants and animals

omen: a prophesy that can be either good or bad

patriarchal society: a society in which men make decisions for the clan or family

predators: animals that live by killing other animals

rondawel: a circular building that has a roof made of thatch and walls made of brick

rural: living in the countryside

urbanized: iving in big towns or cities

vegetarian diet: a diet that does not include meat

FINDING OUT MORE

Books

Cultural Atlas of Africa. Edited by Jocelyn Murray. Amsterdam, the Netherlands: Time Life Books, 1994.

De la Harpe, Roger, and Pat de la Harpe. *Looking at Zulu*. Johannesburg, South Africa: Struik New Holland Publishing, 1998.

Hall, Lynn Bedford. *Shaka Zulu: Warrior King of the Zulu*. Johannesburg, South Africa: Struik New Holland Publishing, 1996.

Holden, Isabella. *The Peace Star/ Inkwenkwezi Yoxolo*. Cape Town, South Africa: Tafelberg Publishers, 1997.

Klopper, Sandra. *The Zulu Kingdom*. Danbury, CT: Franklin Watts, Inc., 1999.

Stotko, Mary-Ann. *Countries of the World: South Africa*. Singapore: Times Editions, 2001.

Videos

Going Places—South Africa. Thirteen WNET New York, 1998.

Websites

<http://www.kwazulu.net/homepage>

<http://www.kwazulunatal.org/kzn>

<http://www.kzn-deat.gov.za/tourism/culture/intro/intro.htm>

<http://www.mambazo.com.zulu>

<http://www.rhino.org.za/our.org>

<http://www.zulu.org.za/kzn>

Organizations

KwaZulu-Natal Nature
Conservation Service
P.O. Box 13053
Cascades, 3202
South Africa
Tel: (27-33) 845-1999
E-mail: <charter@shark.co.za>

KwaZulu-Natal Tourism Authority
P.O. Box 2516
Durban, 4000
South Africa
Tel: (27-31) 207-3728

INDEX

ABOUT THE AUTHORS

Nita Gleimius is currently studying for a degree in ancient Near Eastern cultures and archaeology at the University of South Africa in Pretoria.
Evelina Sibanyoni was raised in a traditional Zulu and Ndebele village, where she learned the ancient arts of basket weaving, pottery, and beadwork. Emma Mthimunye has a Zulu background on her father's side, and Ndebele on her mother's side. She first came into contact with Western culture at the age of seven, when she was sent to a Western-style school in South Africa.

PICTURE CREDITS

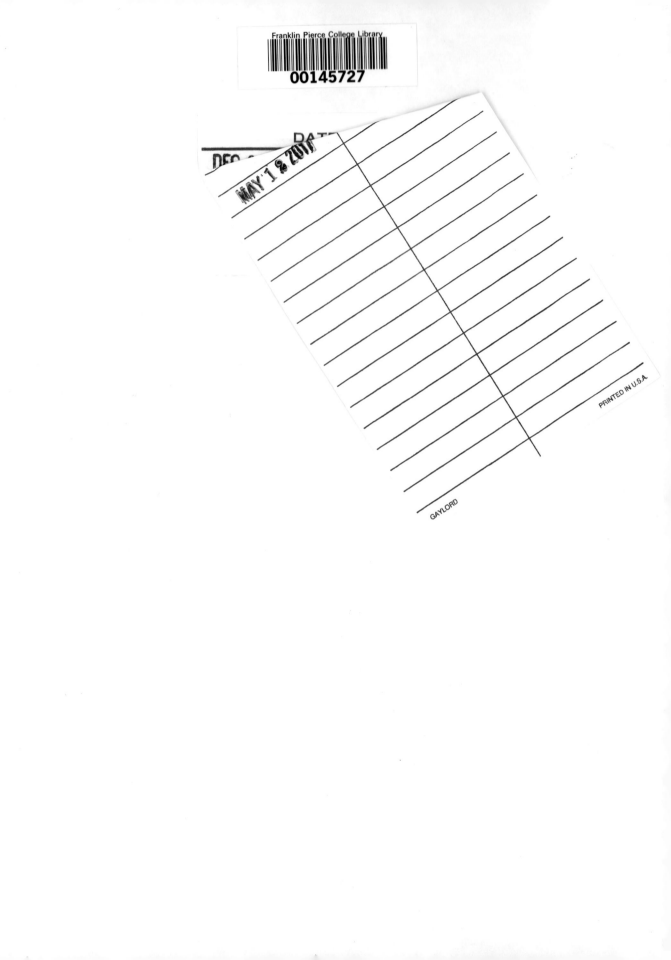